Shadow Work for Couples

A Guide to Strengthen Your Relationship, Build Trust and Understanding, and Cultivate Lasting Love

Callie Parker

Copyright © 2024 by Callie Parker

All rights reserved.

No portion of this book may be reproduced in any form without written permission from the publisher or author, except as permitted by U.S. copyright law.

Download the Audiobook Version for
FREE

If you love listening to audiobooks on-the-go, you can download the audiobook version of this book for FREE just by signing up for a FREE 30-day audible trial!

Scan the QR code or click the links below to get started

>> For Audible US <<

>> For Audible UK <<

>> For Audible FR <<

>> For Audible DE <<

>>For Audible CA<<

>>For Audible AU<<

WELCOME TO
UNLOCKING HAPPINESS
YOUR GUIDE TO ACTIVITIES THAT BOOST YOUR MOOD

Embark on a journey to elevate your daily mood and harness the transformative power of happiness. Inside these pages, you'll discover the scientific underpinnings of how activities can significantly boost your well-being and learn why embracing new experiences is key to a fulfilling life.

What Will You Gain from This eBook?

- Science-Backed Insights
- Practical Strategies
- Daily Habits
- Inspiring Activties
- Creative and Social Pursuits
- Mindfulness and Relaxation Techniques
- Customizable Planner

Ready to Boost Your Happiness? Start your journey now! Scan the QR code or follow the link below to join our newsletter for exclusive content, and begin building your joyful life today.

Send me my free e-book <u>Unlocking Happiness</u>

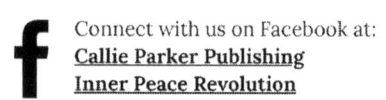

Connect with us on Facebook at:
<u>Callie Parker Publishing</u>
<u>Inner Peace Revolution</u>

MAXIMIZE YOUR SHADOW WORK EXPERIENCE WITH THE COMPANION JOURNAL

Enhance your journey through "Shadow Work for Couples" with this companion journal, designed to deepen your connection and foster shared personal reflection.

- **Deepen Your Shared Understanding:** Engage with exercises that bring clarity and depth to the concepts discussed in the book, allowing for meaningful conversations and mutual growth.
- **Explore Emotions Together:** Create a safe space for both partners to unpack complex emotions privately and openly, fostering greater individual and collective self-awareness.
- **Track Your Progress as a Couple:** Document your growth and discoveries together, creating a valuable resource for future reflection and continued progress as a united front.
- **Customized Exercises for Couples:** Benefit from activities specifically tailored to the unique dynamics of couples, enhancing relevance and impact as you navigate the journey together.

Get your copy of "The Shadow Work Journal for Couples" today and unlock deeper insights into your personal and relational growth.

Contents

Welcome	1
Introduction	3
1. The Unconscious	9
2. Repressed Desires	17
3. Projection	25
4. Integration	31
5. Individuation	37
6. Moral Ambiguity	43
7. Encounter With the Self	49
8. Transformation	55
Afterword	61

Welcome

Welcome to "**Shadow Work for Couples: A Guide to Strengthen Your Relationship, Build Trust and Understanding, and Cultivate Lasting Love**". This book is designed to guide you and your partner on a journey of self-discovery and healing, fostering a deeper, more authentic connection in your relationship.

To enhance your experience, we have created "**The Shadow Work Journal and Workbook for Couples: Heal and Grow Together with Guided Individual and Joint Activities for a Stronger Relationship**". This journal is an essential companion, offering guided activities to help you both apply the concepts discussed in this book and engage in meaningful reflection and exercises together.

We highly recommend using the journal alongside your reading to get the most out of this transformative experience. You can easily access the journal through the following options:

- **Order from Amazon:** Scan the QR code below.

- **Download for Free:** Scan the QR code below.

Introduction

EMBRACING THE JOURNEY TOGETHER

Embarking on a transformative journey of self-discovery and deepened intimacy, this book ventures beyond the surface of conventional relationship advice, diving into the profound teachings of Carl Jung. Our exploration is not just about understanding the individual psyche but about unraveling how these inner worlds shape, challenge, and enrich our intimate partnerships.

In this introduction, we lay the foundation for what lies ahead. We'll begin by demystifying the concept of 'shadow work'—a term that may seem elusive or even intimidating. Here, it becomes a gateway to profound personal growth and relationship enrichment. This journey is not just about confronting the hidden parts of ourselves but also about recognizing how these unseen forces influence our most cherished connections.

Carl Jung, a pioneer in the world of psychology, offered insights that transcend the boundaries of individual therapy. His teachings provide a roadmap for couples eager to explore the depths of their relationship and their own selves. In this book, we weave together Jung's wisdom with practical exercises, creating a unique experience that is both enlightening and deeply personal.

As we embark on this journey, remember that this process is as much about unlearning as it is about learning. It's about peeling back layers of conditioning, societal expectations, and personal defenses to reveal the raw and beautiful truth of who we are and how we love.

This book is designed to be used in conjunction with the Shadow Work Journal for Couples, which offers guided exercises and prompts to complement the theoretical insights provided here. Together, these resources form a cohesive path towards deeper self-awareness and relational harmony.

As you turn these pages, approach this journey with an open heart and mind. Whether you're new to the concept of shadow work or have been exploring your inner landscape for years, this journey is about embracing vulnerability, fostering genuine connection, and nurturing a love that grows deeper and more authentic with each shared experience.

Let's begin this journey of discovery, healing, and connection.

Overview of Carl Jung's Concepts

In the realm of psychological theory, few thinkers have delved as deeply into the mysteries of the human psyche as Carl Gustav Jung. His work, revolutionary and profound, offers a rich tapestry of concepts that have reshaped our understanding of the mind, relationships, and personal growth. This chapter serves as a primer to some of Jung's most significant contributions, setting the stage for their application in the realm of intimate relationships.

1. The Psyche: At the core of Jung's philosophy is the psyche, the total personality that includes consciousness and the unconscious. Jung saw the psyche as a self-regulating system, striving for balance and wholeness. Understanding the dynamics of the psyche is crucial for personal development and relationship harmony.

2. The Conscious and the Unconscious: Jung distinguished between the conscious mind, the part we are aware of, and the vast, often inaccessible unconscious. The unconscious is a reservoir of feelings, thoughts, urges, and memories outside of our conscious awareness. Many of our relationship patterns are rooted in these hidden depths.

3. The Shadow: The shadow is perhaps Jung's most famous concept, referring to the unconscious aspect of the personality which the conscious ego does not identify in itself. It is a repository for traits we deny or dislike in ourselves, which can often surface in relationships in various forms, such as projection.

4. Archetypes: Jung also introduced the idea of archetypes, universal, mythic characters or themes residing in the collective

unconscious. These archetypes, like the Anima and Animus (the feminine image in the male psyche and vice versa), significantly influence our relationships and personal narratives.

5. Individuation: A central process in Jung's theory, individuation is the journey towards wholeness and self-realization. It involves integrating the unconscious with the conscious mind, including the shadow, and is essential for authentic and fulfilling relationships.

6. Synchronicity: Jung's concept of synchronicity, or meaningful coincidences, challenges the notion of random events. Understanding synchronicity can bring a sense of deeper connection and meaning to couples.

7. The Role of Dreams: Dreams, to Jung, were direct messages from the unconscious, helping to guide the individuation process. Interpreting dreams can be a powerful tool for couples to understand their unconscious motivations and fears.

8. Symbolism and Alchemy: Jung saw symbols as key to understanding the unconscious, often using alchemical metaphors to describe psychological processes. The symbolic language can offer couples a unique lens to interpret their experiences and emotions.

This overview of Jung's concepts provides a foundational understanding for the exercises and reflections in this journal. As we delve deeper into each chapter, we will see how these theories apply not just to the individual but in the dance of intimacy and partnership. Understanding Jung's ideas can illuminate the paths we tread in our relationships, offering insights and tools for growth, healing, and deeper connection.

The Importance of Shadow Work in Relationships

Shadow work, a concept derived from the profound insights of Carl Jung, plays a pivotal role in the dynamics of intimate relationships. At its essence, shadow work involves confronting and integrating the parts of ourselves that we have, consciously or unconsciously, rejected or ignored. This chapter delves into why engaging in shadow work is crucial for couples seeking deeper, more authentic connections.

1. Understanding and Acceptance: Relationships often act as mirrors, reflecting our most hidden aspects. Engaging in shadow

work allows individuals in a relationship to understand and accept not only their partner's depths but also their own. This understanding fosters empathy, reduces conflict, and nurtures a deeper sense of acceptance.

2. Reducing Projection: One of the most common challenges in relationships is the tendency to project our own shadow qualities onto our partners. This can lead to misunderstandings and conflicts. Shadow work helps individuals recognize their own projections, leading to healthier and more honest interactions.

3. Authentic Communication: By acknowledging and integrating the shadow, couples can communicate more authentically. This authenticity opens doors to discussing deeper fears, desires, and aspirations, leading to a more profound and meaningful connection.

4. Personal Growth and Relationship Development: Engaging in shadow work is not only beneficial for personal growth but also for the evolution of the relationship. As individuals work through their shadows, they bring more of themselves into the relationship, allowing for a more holistic and dynamic partnership.

5. Breaking Patterns: Many relationship issues are rooted in unresolved personal issues. By addressing these through shadow work, couples can break repetitive, unhealthy patterns, paving the way for more positive dynamics.

6. Enhancing Intimacy: Shadow work can significantly enhance emotional and psychological intimacy. As partners share and explore their shadows together, they build a deeper trust and understanding, strengthening the bond between them.

7. Achieving Balance: Jung believed in the importance of balancing all aspects of the psyche. In relationships, this balance is crucial for harmony. Shadow work helps couples recognize and balance their masculine and feminine energies, leading to a more balanced and fulfilling relationship.

8. Preparing for Life's Challenges: Relationships inevitably face challenges. Couples who have engaged in shadow work are often better equipped to handle life's adversities. Their strengthened communication and understanding provide a solid foundation for navigating difficult times.

In conclusion, shadow work is not merely a journey of individual self-discovery; it's a shared expedition towards a deeper, more resilient partnership. By exploring the shadows together, couples can unlock new levels of understanding, compassion, and connection, enriching their relationship in ways previously unimagined. As we move forward in this book, we'll explore how these concepts can be practically applied to nurture and deepen your intimate bond.

How to Use This Book in Conjunction with the Guided Journal

This shadow work journal for couples is designed as a dual-component journey: a book that provides theoretical insights and a guided journal filled with practical exercises. Used together, they offer a comprehensive approach to exploring the depths of your relationship and individual psyches. Here's how to synergize the use of both components for an enriching experience:

1. Sequential Approach: Start by reading a chapter in the book to gain theoretical understanding. Follow this by engaging with the corresponding chapter in the guided journal. This approach allows the concepts to be freshly in mind when you dive into the exercises.

2. Reflect and Write: After reading each section of the book, take time to reflect on its content. Use the guided journal to express your thoughts, feelings, and any revelations you might have. This process of writing can deepen your understanding and personal connection to the concepts.

3. Shared Learning: Encourage open discussions with your partner about what you've read. This can be done chapter by chapter or at intervals that suit you both. Sharing insights and personal reflections can enhance mutual understanding and empathy.

4. Journal Together: The guided journal exercises are designed to be done both individually and as a couple. Set aside regular times to journal together, discussing your responses and experiences. This shared activity can be a powerful bonding experience and a way to explore your relationship dynamics in real-time.

5. Apply Insights in Daily Life: Try to apply the insights and lessons learned from both the book and the journal in your daily interactions. This practical application is key to making the theoretical knowledge tangible and impactful in your relationship.

6. Revisit and Reflect: Shadow work is an ongoing process. Feel free to revisit chapters and exercises as needed. You may find new insights and understandings emerge at different stages of your relationship.

7. Use Flexiblity: While a sequential approach can be beneficial, feel free to adapt the use of the book and journal to your needs. You may wish to revisit certain chapters or exercises based on what is most relevant to your relationship at a given time.

8. Create a Safe Space: Ensure that both partners feel safe and heard during discussions and journaling sessions. Respect each other's perspectives and use this as an opportunity to deepen trust and intimacy.

By integrating the theoretical knowledge from the book with the introspective and interactive exercises in the guided journal, you and your partner can embark on a meaningful journey of growth and discovery. This journey is about exploring the uncharted territories of your minds and hearts, bringing to light the hidden forces that shape your relationship, and ultimately, forging a deeper, more authentic bond.

The Unconscious

Exploring Hidden Depths for Shared Connection

> "Until you make the unconscious conscious, it will direct your life and you will call it fate." — Carl Jung

In this chapter, we delve into one of Carl Jung's most profound and influential concepts: the unconscious. This exploration is not just an academic exercise; it's a journey to the depths of our own psyche and that of our partner. Understanding the unconscious is pivotal in grasping the undercurrents that shape our behaviors, reactions, and interactions within our relationships.

The unconscious mind, as conceptualized by Jung, is a vast reservoir of feelings, thoughts, memories, and desires that lie outside of our conscious awareness. It's the hidden domain of our psyche, holding the keys to understanding the intricate dance of our emotions and actions. In the context of a relationship, the unconscious becomes even more significant, often dictating the rhythm and patterns of our interactions with our partner, sometimes in ways we are not immediately aware of.

In this chapter, we will:
- Explore the Landscape of the Unconscious: We will begin by mapping out the terrain of the unconscious mind, understanding its structure and how it differs from the conscious mind. This exploration will include an examination of Jung's theory of the personal and collective

unconscious.

- Uncover the Role of the Unconscious in Relationships: We'll investigate how the unconscious influences our romantic relationships. This includes how our hidden fears, desires, and past experiences shape the way we love, argue, and connect.

- Identify Unconscious Influences: Through various examples and analyses, we'll learn how to identify the signs of unconscious influences in our daily interactions. This knowledge is crucial for understanding and navigating the complexities of intimate relationships.

- Understand the Power of the Unconscious: We'll delve into the transformative power of bringing unconscious elements into conscious awareness. This process is essential for personal growth and the development of a healthy, fulfilling relationship.

This chapter aims to equip you with a deeper understanding of the unseen forces at play in your relationship. As you read, you will gain insights that will illuminate your interactions, helping you and your partner to navigate the often mysterious and powerful realm of the unconscious with greater awareness and empathy.

Explanation of the Unconscious Mind According to Jung

Carl Jung's exploration of the unconscious mind marked a significant departure from the prevailing psychological theories of his time. He viewed the unconscious not as a mere repository of repressed desires and traumas, but as a rich, dynamic component of our psyche integral to our psychological processes. This section delves into Jung's understanding of the unconscious, illuminating its complexities and significance.

1. The Personal Unconscious: Jung identified the personal unconscious as a layer of the psyche containing thoughts and feelings not immediately present in consciousness. This includes forgotten experiences, repressed memories, subliminal

perceptions, and undeveloped ideas. According to Jung, these elements can influence our behavior and emotional responses, often in ways we do not consciously recognize.

2. The Collective Unconscious: Beyond the personal unconscious, Jung introduced the concept of the collective unconscious. This is a deeper level shared by all individuals, holding the universal experiences of humanity. It contains archetypes, which are innate, universal psychic dispositions that form the substrate from which the basic themes of human life emerge.

3. Archetypes: Within the collective unconscious, archetypes like the Shadow, the Anima and Animus, the Mother, the Hero, and the Wise Old Man, play a crucial role. They represent fundamental human motifs and can manifest in dreams, fantasies, and behavior. In relationships, these archetypes can influence how we perceive and interact with our partners.

4. Dreams as a Window to the Unconscious: Jung believed that dreams are a direct pathway to the unconscious. They serve as a bridge between the conscious and unconscious realms, offering insights and messages that, if interpreted, can lead to profound self-awareness and understanding.

5. Symbols and the Unconscious: Jung also emphasized the importance of symbols, viewing them as manifestations of unconscious processes. Symbols, he argued, are the language of the unconscious, and deciphering them can unlock deeper understanding of our psyche and our relationships.

6. The Role of the Unconscious in Personality Development: Jung saw the interaction between the conscious and unconscious mind as vital for psychological growth. This process, known as individuation, involves integrating the unconscious aspects of the psyche into conscious awareness, leading to a more balanced and whole individual.

In essence, Jung's view of the unconscious offers a rich, multi-layered understanding of the human psyche. It suggests that our behaviors, feelings, and relationship dynamics are profoundly influenced by unconscious processes. By exploring and integrating these unconscious elements, we open the door to greater self-awareness, personal growth, and a deeper, more meaningful connection in our intimate relationships.

The Role of the Unconscious in Romantic Relationships

The unconscious mind, as conceptualized by Carl Jung, plays a crucial yet often understated role in shaping the dynamics of romantic relationships. This invisible undercurrent of our psyche influences how we connect, react, and engage with our partners, often steering the course of a relationship in profound ways. Understanding the role of the unconscious can illuminate many aspects of romantic partnerships, from the initial spark of attraction to the deeper aspects of long-term bonding.

1. Attraction and the Unconscious: The initial attraction between individuals is often influenced by unconscious factors. Jungian psychology suggests that we are drawn to partners who unconsciously remind us of aspects of our parents or primary caregivers, seeking to heal unresolved childhood dynamics. This phenomenon, often referred to as transference, can play a significant role in our choice of partners.

2. Projection in Relationships: One of the most significant roles of the unconscious in relationships is the projection of our own shadow qualities onto our partner. We may attribute negative traits or qualities to our partners, which are actually aspects of ourselves that we have not fully acknowledged or integrated. Recognizing and understanding these projections can lead to healthier and more authentic relationships.

3. The Dance of Anima and Animus: According to Jung, each person carries within them both masculine and feminine qualities – the animus (the masculine inner personality in women) and the anima (the feminine inner personality in men). In relationships, individuals often project their anima or animus onto their partner. This projection can either enrich the relationship by bringing balance or cause misunderstandings and conflicts if not recognized and managed.

4. Unconscious Communication: Much of our communication in relationships operates on an unconscious level. Non-verbal cues, emotional reactions, and even our expectations are often governed by unconscious processes. By becoming more aware of these unconscious elements, couples can develop a deeper understanding and connection.

5. Repetition Compulsion: Jungian psychology highlights how individuals often unconsciously repeat patterns of behavior in relationships. These patterns, rooted in past experiences and unprocessed emotions, can lead to cycles of conflict or dissatisfaction. By bringing these patterns into conscious awareness, couples can break free from them and foster healthier dynamics.

6. Healing and Growth through Relationships: Romantic relationships offer a unique opportunity for personal growth and healing. The unconscious mind often guides us towards partners who can help us confront and integrate our shadow aspects. This process, though challenging, can lead to significant personal transformation and a more profound relationship experience.

Understanding the role of the unconscious in romantic relationships is not just about uncovering hidden motives or resolving past traumas. It's about deepening the connection with our partners, fostering mutual growth, and navigating the complex but rewarding journey of love with greater awareness and empathy. As we explore the nuances of the unconscious, we become better equipped to cultivate relationships that are not only loving but also transformative.

Case Studies and Stories

To further illustrate the role of the unconscious in romantic relationships, this section presents a series of case studies and stories. These real-life examples offer a window into how unconscious dynamics play out in relationships, providing insights and lessons that can be applied in your own journey of love and self-discovery.

1. The Story of Emma and Tom: Emma and Tom's relationship was marked by frequent arguments about commitment. Through therapy, they discovered that Emma had an unconscious fear of abandonment stemming from her father's early departure in her life. This fear was causing her to push Tom for more commitment, which in turn triggered Tom's unconscious fear of being controlled, rooted in his relationship with his overbearing mother. Recognizing these unconscious influences allowed them to approach their relationship with more empathy and understanding.

2. The Case of Sarah and Alex: Sarah often felt neglected in her relationship with Alex, believing he was emotionally unavailable. A deeper exploration revealed that Sarah was projecting her shadow qualities of emotional detachment onto Alex. In reality, Sarah struggled with vulnerability due to past traumas. As she worked on integrating these aspects of her shadow, their relationship dynamics improved significantly.

3. The Transformation of Mike and Linda: Mike and Linda sought help for what they believed was a lack of passion in their relationship. Through guided shadow work, they discovered that they were both projecting their anima and animus onto each other, expecting the other to fulfill unrealistic ideals. By acknowledging and integrating these projections, they found a renewed sense of passion and intimacy.

4. The Healing Journey of Rachel and David: Rachel and David's relationship was strained due to David's infidelity. Through couples therapy focusing on Jungian concepts, they unearthed that David's actions were partly driven by unconscious patterns he inherited from his father's behavior. Addressing these patterns was key to healing and rebuilding their relationship.

5. The Story of Anita and Chris: Anita and Chris struggled with communication issues. Anita felt that Chris was not open with his feelings. Through shadow work, Chris uncovered that his reluctance to express emotions was linked to an unconscious belief that men should not show vulnerability. Recognizing and challenging this belief led to more open and honest communication between them.

These case studies and stories demonstrate the profound impact of the unconscious on romantic relationships. They show how uncovering and understanding unconscious patterns, fears, and desires can lead to healing, growth, and a deeper connection between partners. Each story is a testament to the transformative power of self-awareness and the courage to face the hidden aspects of ourselves and our relationships.

***

- Turn to the corresponding section in *The Shadow Work Journal and Workbook for Couples* and complete the exercises. Reflect on your insights, apply the concepts, and explore your personal experiences. Taking this time for self-reflection will enhance your journey.

Repressed Desires

UNVEILING HIDDEN ASPECTS FOR A FULFILLING BOND

> "What you resist, persists." — Carl Jung

In Chapter 2, "Repressed Desires," we explore one of the most intriguing yet often misunderstood aspects of our psyche and relationships: the realm of desires that we have pushed into the shadows of our unconscious. Repressed desires are those wishes, needs, and fantasies that, for various reasons, we have learned to hide or suppress. These can range from personal ambitions to emotional needs, sexual fantasies, or even aspects of our personality that we feel are unacceptable.

Jungian psychology offers a profound lens through which to understand the nature and impact of these repressed desires. In the context of romantic relationships, these hidden desires can play a significant role, often surfacing indirectly and influencing our interactions in ways we might not consciously recognize.

In this chapter, we will:
- Define Repressed Desires: We will begin by understanding what repressed desires are and how they differ from our conscious wishes and wants. This includes exploring the mechanisms of repression and the reasons why certain desires become repressed.

- The Impact on Relationships: Repressed desires can have

a significant impact on romantic relationships. They can manifest as unexplained dissatisfaction, unfulfilled needs, or inexplicable attractions and aversions. Understanding this impact is crucial for addressing underlying issues in a relationship.

- Identifying Repressed Desires: Through case studies and reflective exercises, we will explore how to identify signs of repressed desires within ourselves and our partners. This understanding is the first step towards bringing these desires into conscious awareness.

- Jung's Perspective on Desire and the Psyche: Carl Jung's insights into the nature of desire and its relationship with the other parts of the psyche provide a valuable framework for understanding and integrating repressed desires.

- The Role of Repressed Desires in Personal Growth: We will delve into how acknowledging and integrating repressed desires can be a transformative process, leading to greater self-awareness, personal growth, and fulfillment.

- Transforming Relationships through Integrating Desires: Finally, we will explore how couples can work together to recognize and integrate repressed desires, leading to a more authentic, satisfying, and dynamic relationship.

"Repressed Desires" is a chapter that invites both introspection and open dialogue between partners. It offers a journey into the deeper, often unexplored territories of our hearts and minds, revealing how the shadows of our desires shape the landscape of our relationships. By confronting and embracing these hidden parts of ourselves, we open the door to a more profound and genuine connection with our partners.

Understanding Repressed Desires and Their Impact on Relationships

Understanding repressed desires and their impact on relationships is crucial for fostering deeper, more authentic connections between partners. Repressed desires are those aspects of our emotional and psychological makeup that, for various reasons, we have unconsciously chosen to hide or ignore. These can include unacknowledged emotional needs, suppressed aspirations, or forbidden impulses.

1. Nature of Repressed Desires: Repressed desires often stem from early life experiences, cultural conditioning, or personal fears. They are the wishes, emotions, and needs that we have pushed out of our conscious awareness, usually because they conflict with our self-image or societal expectations.

2. Repression as a Defense Mechanism: Repression serves as a psychological defense mechanism to avoid dealing with uncomfortable or painful emotions. While it can provide short-term relief or stability, over time, these repressed desires can exert a significant influence on behavior and emotional well-being.

3. Impact on Personal Behavior: Individuals with repressed desires might experience unexplained mood swings, irrational reactions, or persistent feelings of dissatisfaction. These internal conflicts can also manifest as physical symptoms, a phenomenon known as psychosomatic response.

4. Influence on Relationship Dynamics: In romantic relationships, repressed desires can lead to various issues:
- Projection: Individuals may project their unacknowledged desires onto their partners, misinterpreting their partner's actions or words.

- Conflict and Misunderstanding: Misalignment between conscious behaviors and unconscious desires can create conflict, leading to arguments and misunderstandings.

- Emotional Distance: Repressing significant desires can create a barrier to emotional intimacy, as one is not fully present or authentic in the relationship.

5. Recognizing Repressed Desires: Identifying repressed desires requires introspection and often, external help such as therapy. Signs include consistent patterns of dissatisfaction, unexplained emotional reactions, or a feeling of 'something missing' in one's life or relationships.

6. Integrating Repressed Desires: Addressing and integrating repressed desires involves bringing them into conscious

awareness, understanding their origins, and finding healthy ways to acknowledge and express them. This process can lead to personal healing and growth.

7. Positive Transformation in Relationships: As individuals work through their repressed desires, they often find that their relationships improve. This improvement comes from increased self-awareness, more authentic communication, and a deeper understanding of each other's needs and desires.

In summary, repressed desires can have a profound impact on both individual well-being and the health of romantic relationships. Acknowledging, understanding, and integrating these desires are key steps towards personal fulfillment and relationship harmony. This journey, while challenging, can lead to a deeper connection and a more authentic partnership.

Jung's Perspective on Desire and the Psyche

Within the framework of Carl Jung's exploration of the unconscious, his perspective on desire holds a significant place. Jung viewed the realm of desire as an essential component of the psyche, intricately linked with both conscious and unconscious processes. This understanding provides valuable insights into how repressed desires can shape our relationships and personal growth.

1. Desire in the Context of the Psyche: Jung saw desire as a fundamental human experience, deeply rooted in both the conscious and unconscious mind. He recognized that while some desires are openly acknowledged and pursued, others are repressed, often relegated to the shadows of the unconscious.

2. The Shadow and Repressed Desires: Central to Jung's theory is the concept of the Shadow, the part of the psyche where traits and desires deemed unacceptable or threatening to the ego are stored. These repressed desires, hidden in the Shadow, can significantly influence behavior and choices, albeit unconsciously. For Jung, confronting and integrating these shadow aspects was crucial for achieving psychological balance and wholeness.

3. The Process of Individuation and Desire: The integration of repressed desires is integral to what Jung termed the individuation process – a journey towards self-realization and completeness. This process involves recognizing and reconciling

the disparate parts of the self, including those desires that have been suppressed or ignored.

4. Desire and Projection in Relationships: In romantic relationships, Jung's theory illuminates how unacknowledged desires can lead to projection, where one partner may attribute their repressed desires or qualities to the other. This dynamic can lead to misunderstandings and conflicts, making the recognition and integration of these desires crucial for relationship harmony.

5. The Transformative Power of Acknowledging Desire: Jung believed that acknowledging and integrating repressed desires could lead to significant personal transformation. This transformation is not limited to individual growth but extends to the dynamics of romantic relationships, where a deeper understanding of one's desires can lead to more authentic and fulfilling connections.

In summary, Jung's perspective on desire and the psyche offers a nuanced understanding of the complex interplay between our innermost wishes and our conscious life, particularly in the context of intimate relationships. By exploring these hidden desires, individuals can embark on a path of self-discovery and relational depth, unlocking new levels of understanding and connection.

The Difference Between Healthy and Unhealthy Repression

In exploring the dynamics of the unconscious, particularly in the context of repressed desires, it's essential to distinguish between healthy and unhealthy repression. Carl Jung's theories provide a framework for understanding this differentiation, which is crucial in personal development and the health of romantic relationships.

1. Healthy Repression as a Psychological Mechanism: Healthy repression can be understood as a natural psychological process where certain desires or impulses are unconsciously set aside to maintain social appropriateness, psychological balance, and focus. This type of repression is temporary and adaptive, helping us to function effectively in various social and personal contexts.

2. Unhealthy Repression and its Consequences: Unhealthy repression occurs when desires and emotions are chronically pushed into the unconscious, often due to fear, trauma, or

societal norms. These repressed elements do not disappear but can manifest in various disruptive ways, such as anxiety, depression, relationship conflicts, or even physical symptoms. Unresolved, these repressed elements can significantly hinder personal growth and relational satisfaction.

3. Repression in Relationships: In the context of relationships, unhealthy repression often leads to misunderstandings, resentment, and a lack of intimacy. For example, if a partner represses their need for emotional closeness due to fear of vulnerability, this can create distance and disconnection in the relationship

4. Jung's View on Repression and Individuation: Jung emphasized that recognizing and integrating repressed aspects of the self is vital for the process of individuation – the journey toward wholeness. This integration includes acknowledging repressed desires, which can lead to a more authentic and fulfilling life, including healthier relationship dynamics.

5. Identifying and Addressing Unhealthy Repression: The key to transforming unhealthy repression into a path of growth lies in self-awareness and often, therapeutic intervention. This involves exploring the unconscious, understanding the origins of repressed desires, and gradually integrating these aspects into conscious awareness.

6. The Role of Dreams and Symbols: Jung believed that dreams and symbolic imagery could provide insights into repressed aspects of the psyche. By analyzing dreams and symbols, individuals can gain access to repressed desires and begin the process of integrating them.

In summary, the distinction between healthy and unhealthy repression is crucial in understanding the role of the unconscious in personal and relational well-being. Recognizing and addressing unhealthy repression can lead to significant improvements in emotional health, personal growth, and the quality of romantic relationships. The next sections will delve deeper into how individuals and couples can identify and work through unhealthy repression, paving the way for more authentic and fulfilling connections.

***

- Turn to the corresponding section in *The Shadow Work Journal and Workbook for Couples* and complete the exercises. Reflect on your insights, apply the concepts, and explore your personal experiences. Taking this time for self-reflection will enhance your journey.

Projection

Understanding Ourselves, Understanding Each Other

> "Everything that irritates us about others can lead us to an understanding of ourselves." — Carl Jung

In Chapter 3, "Projection," we embark on an exploration of one of the most intriguing and impactful phenomena in relationships: the projection of our own unconscious aspects onto our partners. This concept, rooted in Jungian psychology, reveals how we often attribute our own repressed feelings, desires, and fears to those closest to us, particularly our romantic partners. Understanding and navigating this complex psychological terrain is key to fostering healthier and more authentic relationships.

Projection occurs when an individual unconsciously transfers their own attributes, emotions, or desires onto someone else. In the context of a romantic relationship, this can lead to misunderstandings, conflicts, and a distorted view of the partner. For instance, one might accuse their partner of being angry or distant, when in fact, these are the qualities they are uncomfortable acknowledging in themselves.

This chapter will cover several key areas:
- Defining Projection: A clear understanding of what projection is and how it operates within the psyche and relationships.

- Examples of Projection in Relationships: Real-life scenarios and case studies illustrating how projection manifests in romantic partnerships.

- The Origins of Projection: Delving into the psychological roots of projection, including its ties to repressed aspects of the self and unacknowledged emotions.

- Consequences of Projection: Examining how unchecked projection can lead to relationship strain, miscommunication, and emotional distance.

- Differentiating Self from Other: Learning to recognize and differentiate between one's own feelings and attributes and those truly belonging to the partner.

- Navigating and Resolving Projection: Practical strategies for couples to identify, confront, and work through projections, enhancing understanding and intimacy.

"Projection" promises to be a chapter rich in insight, guiding readers through the often-subtle ways our unconscious mind influences our perceptions and interactions. By shedding light on this phenomenon, couples can move towards a more honest and empathetic understanding of each other, transforming potential conflicts into opportunities for growth and deeper connection.

Concept of Projection in Psychology

The concept of projection in psychology, particularly as developed by Carl Jung, is integral to understanding both personal behavior and interpersonal dynamics. Projection occurs when an individual subconsciously transfers their own unacceptable qualities, feelings, or motivations onto someone else, typically without awareness of doing so. This mechanism serves as a defense strategy, shielding the individual from acknowledging qualities they find difficult to accept in themselves.

- Basic Definition of Projection: Projection involves attributing one's own repressed feelings, desires, or impulses to another person, often leading to a distortion of reality. For instance, someone who is untrusting might accuse their partner of being deceitful.

- Jung's Perspective on Projection: Carl Jung viewed projection as a natural part of the human psyche's functioning. It's a defense mechanism that occurs when the individual's ego defends itself against unconscious impulses or qualities, either positive or negative, by denying their existence in themselves while attributing them to others.

- Projection and the Shadow: Projection is closely linked to Jung's concept of the Shadow, which comprises the parts of our personality that we reject or deem unacceptable. When these shadow aspects are not consciously acknowledged, they can be projected onto others, particularly close partners in a romantic relationship.

- Projection in Relationships: In the context of romantic relationships, projection can lead to significant misunderstandings and conflicts. For example, an individual might project their own feelings of inadequacy onto their partner, perceiving them as critical or unsupportive, when in fact, these feelings originate within themselves.

- Recognizing and Addressing Projection: The process of recognizing and addressing projection involves self-reflection and introspection. It requires individuals to look inward to understand their own feelings and motivations, rather than attributing them to their partner.

- Therapeutic Approaches to Projection: In therapeutic settings, techniques such as open dialogue, mindfulness practices, and dream analysis are often used to help individuals recognize and work through their projections.

In summary, understanding the concept of projection is crucial for personal growth and the development of healthy, authentic relationships. Recognizing when and how we project onto our partners can lead to more honest and empathetic interactions, paving the way for a deeper understanding of ourselves and our relationships. The next sections will delve deeper into the mechanics of projection in romantic relationships and provide practical guidance for identifying and overcoming this psychological phenomenon.

How Couples Project Onto Each Other

Projection in couples is a common phenomenon and understanding it can profoundly impact the health and dynamics of a relationship. When partners project, they are essentially seeing in each other aspects of themselves that they are not fully conscious of or comfortable with. This can lead to a complex interplay of emotions and behaviors that, if not understood and managed, can create barriers to intimacy and understanding.

- Projection of Unresolved Personal Issues: Often, individuals project unresolved personal issues onto their partners. For example, a person with unresolved abandonment issues might perceive their partner as distant or uncommitted, even when this is not the case.

- Projection of Shadow Aspects: Partners may project their shadow aspects – those parts of their personality they reject or don't acknowledge – onto each other. For instance, if one partner struggles with feelings of jealousy but does not recognize this trait in themselves, they may accuse their partner of being jealous.

- Repetition of Past Patterns: Many times, individuals unconsciously project roles or dynamics from their past onto their partners. A person may, for instance, project the characteristics of a parent onto their partner, replaying old family dynamics in the relationship.

- Deflection of Own Feelings: Projection can also be a way to deflect uncomfortable feelings about oneself. A partner might accuse the other of being angry or unhappy as a way to avoid confronting their own anger or unhappiness.

- Triggering Each Other's Projections: In a relationship, partners can trigger each other's projections, often unknowingly. One partner's behavior may activate unresolved issues in the other, leading to a cycle of projection and reaction.

- Recognizing and Managing Projections: It is important for couples to learn to recognize when they are projecting. This often involves honest self-reflection and open communication. Acknowledging and discussing these projections can lead to greater understanding and intimacy.

Understanding how projection works in relationships is a crucial step towards healthier and more genuine connections. It encourages partners to look inward, to understand their own psyche better, and to communicate more effectively with each other. The journey to recognizing and managing projections can be challenging but is deeply rewarding, leading to a more empathetic and authentic relationship.

Recognizing and Managing Projections in a Relationship

Recognizing and managing projections is a vital skill for maintaining a healthy, authentic relationship. Projections can distort perceptions and create misunderstandings, leading to conflicts and a lack of genuine connection. Here are some key aspects of recognizing and managing projections in a relationship:

- Signs of Projection: The first step in managing projections is to recognize their occurrence. Signs include strong emotional reactions to a partner's behavior, seeing one's own unacknowledged traits in the partner, and repeated patterns of blame or criticism.

- Self-Reflection and Awareness: Self-awareness is crucial in identifying projections. It involves reflecting on one's feelings and reactions and asking whether they are truly about the partner or reflective of one's own internal issues.

- Open Communication: Once a projection is recognized, it's important to communicate openly about it. This doesn't mean accusing the partner of causing these feelings, but rather sharing one's own process of realization and the emotions that arise.

- Understanding the Origin of Projections: Understanding where projections come from – often past experiences, unresolved conflicts, or aspects of the shadow self – is key to managing them. This understanding can come through self-reflection, therapy, or even open discussions with the partner.

- Developing Empathy: Developing empathy for one's partner is essential in overcoming projections. This means trying to understand the partner's perspective and feelings without the distortion of one's own projected issues.

- Joint Efforts in Overcoming Projections: Managing projections in a relationship is not a solitary task. It involves both partners working together to understand and address the underlying issues, supporting each other in the process.

- Professional Help: Sometimes, external help from a therapist or counselor can provide the necessary guidance to recognize and manage projections effectively, especially if they are deeply rooted.

By recognizing and managing projections, couples can move towards a more honest and understanding relationship. This process not only improves the dynamics of the relationship but also contributes to each individual's personal growth and self-awareness.

***

- Turn to the corresponding section in *The Shadow Work Journal and Workbook for Couples* and complete the exercises. Reflect on your insights, apply the concepts, and explore your personal experiences. Taking this time for self-reflection will enhance your journey.

Integration

HARMONIZING THE SHADOW FOR RELATIONSHIP WHOLENESS

> "Your visions will become clear only when you can look into your own heart. Who looks outside, dreams; who looks inside, awakes." — Carl Jung

Chapter 4, "Integration," delves into a crucial aspect of Jungian psychology and its application to relationships: the integration of the shadow. This process involves recognizing, accepting, and incorporating the disowned and unconscious aspects of ourselves into our conscious identity. In the context of a romantic relationship, integration is essential for authenticity, emotional intimacy, and relational harmony.

In this chapter, we explore the journey of acknowledging our shadow aspects, understanding their influence on our behavior and relationships, and learning how to integrate these parts constructively. Integration is not about eliminating the shadow but about transforming our relationship with it, leading to greater self-understanding and a more harmonious partnership.

Through the lens of Jungian psychology, this chapter will guide you and your partner on a path of self-discovery. By embracing the parts of ourselves we have previously ignored or suppressed, we open the door to profound personal growth and deeper, more authentic connections with our partners. Integration is a key step towards a relationship that is not only loving but also deeply rooted in mutual understanding and acceptance.

The Process of Integrating the Shadow

Integrating the shadow is a fundamental process in Jungian psychology, essential for personal growth and the development of healthy, authentic relationships. It involves recognizing and embracing the parts of ourselves that we have consciously or unconsciously rejected or ignored. This process is not only transformative for individuals but also deeply impacts the dynamics within a romantic relationship.

- Acknowledgment of the Shadow: The first step in shadow integration is acknowledging its existence. This involves an honest self-assessment to recognize the traits, impulses, and emotions that one has been denying or repressing.

- Understanding the Shadow: Gaining insight into the nature of one's shadow is crucial. This includes exploring its origins—often rooted in early life experiences—and understanding how it has influenced one's behavior and relationship patterns.

- Acceptance and Compassion: Accepting the shadow involves a non-judgmental acknowledgment of these repressed parts. It requires a compassionate attitude towards oneself, understanding that these aspects, no matter how challenging, are part of the human experience.

- Dialogue with the Shadow: Engaging in an inner dialogue with the shadow can be a powerful tool for integration. This might involve reflective practices such as journaling, meditation, or therapy, where one consciously communicates with and listens to the shadow.

- Transformative Practices: Practical steps for integrating the shadow include mindfulness exercises, artistic expression, and therapeutic techniques. These practices help in bringing the shadow into consciousness and finding constructive ways to express these repressed aspects.

- Impact on Relationships: In relationships, shadow integration can lead to a reduction in projection, fewer conflicts, and a deeper level of understanding and empathy between partners. By owning one's shadow, individuals can interact with their partners more authentically and compassionately.

- Ongoing Process: Integration is not a one-time event but an ongoing process. It requires continuous self-awareness and effort to maintain the balance between the conscious and unconscious aspects of the self.

Integrating the shadow is a journey towards embracing the full spectrum of one's personality. It allows individuals to be more whole and authentic, both within themselves and in their relationships. This chapter provides a roadmap for understanding and engaging in this transformative process, highlighting its profound impact on personal well-being and the quality of romantic partnerships.

Benefits of Integration in Personal and Relationship Growth

The integration of the shadow, a concept central to Jungian psychology, offers significant benefits for both personal development and the growth of relationships. By embracing and integrating the shadow—the repressed, ignored, or undeclared aspects of our personality—we can achieve a more complete and authentic self. This process has profound implications not just for individual well-being but also for the health and depth of romantic relationships.

- Enhanced Self-Awareness: Integrating the shadow leads to greater self-awareness. Understanding the full range of one's emotions, motivations, and desires, including those previously hidden in the shadow, allows for a more authentic and complete sense of self.

- Improved Self-Acceptance: As individuals recognize and accept their shadow aspects, they develop a more compassionate and accepting attitude toward themselves.

This self-acceptance is crucial for personal well-being and self-esteem.

- Reduction of Projection: A significant benefit in relationships is the reduction of projection. When individuals acknowledge their own shadow aspects, they are less likely to project these qualities onto their partners, leading to fewer misunderstandings and conflicts.

- Deeper Emotional Intimacy: The process of shadow integration encourages vulnerability and honesty. As partners share and accept not only their strengths but also their weaknesses and fears, they develop deeper emotional intimacy and trust.

- More Authentic Relationships: Integration allows individuals to show up in their relationships more authentically. When both partners embrace their whole selves, the relationship is based on genuine understanding and acceptance.

- Personal Growth and Maturity: Integrating the shadow is a key step in personal development and maturity. It involves facing uncomfortable truths, challenging ingrained patterns, and growing beyond them.

- Enhanced Relationship Dynamics: As individuals become more integrated and whole, their relationships naturally become healthier and more balanced. This can lead to a more harmonious and fulfilling partnership.

- Conflict Resolution: With a deeper understanding of themselves and their partners, individuals are better equipped to navigate and resolve conflicts in a constructive manner.

In conclusion, the integration of the shadow is a transformative process that yields significant benefits for both individuals and their relationships. It fosters a level of authenticity, understanding, and connection that forms the foundation of a strong, healthy, and evolving relationship.

Techniques and Examples from Jung's Work

Carl Jung's work provides various techniques for integrating the shadow, each designed to bring unconscious aspects into conscious awareness. These methods not only aid in personal growth but also offer profound insights that can enhance relationship dynamics. Here are some of Jung's key techniques, accompanied by examples to illustrate their application:

- Active Imagination: This technique involves engaging with the unconscious in a meditative state. It allows individuals to dialogue with different aspects of their psyche, including the shadow. For instance, Jung would often encourage patients to converse with their dreams' characters, treating them as real entities with their own voices and stories.

- Dream Analysis: Jung saw dreams as direct communications from the unconscious. Analyzing dreams can provide insights into one's shadow. For example, a dream where one is being chased might reveal aspects of the self that the dreamer is running away from or ignoring.

- Symbolic Representation: Artistic expressions such as drawing, painting, or sculpting can be used to represent and explore aspects of the shadow. For instance, creating a piece of art that embodies a repressed emotion can help in understanding and integrating that emotion.

- Journaling: Writing about thoughts, feelings, and dreams can help bring clarity to the shadow aspects. Jung himself kept a detailed Red Book where he recorded his dreams and active imaginations, which was instrumental in his process of self-discovery and development of his theories.

- Exploring Archetypes: Engaging with the universal archetypes identified by Jung (such as the Hero, the Shadow, the Anima/Animus) can illuminate aspects of the shadow. For example, recognizing the traits of the 'Anima' or 'Animus' in oneself can reveal how gender dynamics influence one's personality and relationships.

- Therapeutic Dialogue: In therapy, discussing personal history and recurring patterns can uncover shadow elements. Therapists trained in Jungian psychology often use a patient's narratives and experiences as a gateway to exploring their unconscious.

- Meditation and Mindfulness: Practices like meditation and mindfulness create space for self-reflection and awareness, crucial for acknowledging and integrating the shadow.

- Individuation Process: This overarching journey involves continuously striving to balance and integrate all parts of the psyche, including the shadow, into a cohesive whole.

These techniques, rooted in Jung's profound understanding of the human psyche, offer valuable pathways for individuals seeking to integrate their shadow. In turn, this integration significantly benefits personal growth and the health of intimate relationships. Through these practices, individuals can achieve a greater sense of wholeness, authenticity, and connection with themselves and their partners.

***

- Turn to the corresponding section in *The Shadow Work Journal and Workbook for Couples* and complete the exercises. Reflect on your insights, apply the concepts, and explore your personal experiences. Taking this time for self-reflection will enhance your journey.

Individuation

FOSTERING INDIVIDUAL GROWTH WITHIN A UNIFIED PARTNERSHIP

> "Individuation means becoming a single, homogeneous being, and, in so far as 'individuality' embraces our innermost, last, and incomparable uniqueness, it also implies becoming one's own self." — Carl Jung

Chapter 5, "Individuation," focuses on one of Carl Jung's most significant contributions to psychology and personal development. Individuation is the process of becoming aware of oneself and integrating different aspects of one's personality to become a whole and individual person. This journey is not just about personal growth; it's crucial for the development of healthy, authentic relationships.

In a relationship context, individuation involves both partners growing into their most authentic selves, which paradoxically allows for a deeper, more genuine connection with each other. This chapter delves into the journey towards individuation, examining how it affects each individual and the relationship as a unit.

This exploration will provide insight into the balancing act between personal growth and relational harmony. It will guide couples through the complexities of supporting each other's individual journeys while nurturing their shared path. Understanding and engaging in the process of individuation can lead to a more fulfilling and meaningful partnership, where both individuals feel seen, heard, and valued for their true selves.

The Journey Towards Individuation

The journey towards individuation is a core concept in Jungian psychology, representing a process of self-discovery and personal development. It involves integrating various aspects of the personality to achieve a sense of wholeness. This journey is not just an individual endeavor; in the context of a romantic relationship, it plays a crucial role in how partners relate to and understand each other.

- Understanding the Self: Individuation begins with a deep understanding of oneself. This includes recognizing and accepting one's strengths, weaknesses, desires, fears, and the unconscious aspects of the psyche.

- Confronting the Shadow: A key part of individuation involves confronting the shadow, the unacknowledged or rejected parts of one's personality. This step is crucial for growth as it prevents projecting these aspects onto the partner.

- Integration of Opposites: Individuation involves reconciling the opposing forces within the psyche, such as the masculine and feminine aspects (animus and anima), rational and irrational tendencies, and conscious and unconscious elements.

- Developing Personal Autonomy: Through individuation, individuals develop greater autonomy and a clearer sense of their values and beliefs. This autonomy allows for healthier and more balanced relationships.

- The Role of Dreams and Symbols: Dreams and symbols play a significant role in the individuation process. They can provide insights into the deeper aspects of the psyche and guide personal growth.

- Ongoing Process: Individuation is not a destination but an ongoing journey of self-exploration and development. It evolves over time, paralleling one's life experiences and relationships.

- Impact on Relationships: As individuals journey towards individuation, their relationships can become more authentic and profound. Partners who engage in their individuation processes can support each other's growth, leading to a more harmonious and fulfilling partnership.

- Navigating Relationship Dynamics: The process of individuation requires individuals to navigate the dynamics of their relationship carefully, ensuring that personal growth enhances rather than conflicts with the relationship.

In sum, the journey towards individuation is a deeply personal yet relationally significant path. It fosters self-awareness, personal growth, and a deeper, more genuine connection with one's partner. For couples, understanding and supporting each other on this journey can be a profound source of strength and harmony in the relationship.

Balancing Individuation and Intimacy in Relationships

Balancing the journey of individuation with maintaining intimacy in a relationship is a delicate and essential task. Individuation, the process of becoming an integrated and fully realized individual, can sometimes seem at odds with the closeness and shared identity that a relationship fosters. However, when navigated thoughtfully, these two paths can complement and enrich each other.

- Understanding the Interplay: It's important to understand that individuation and intimacy are not mutually exclusive. In fact, a more individuated self can lead to deeper, more authentic intimacy. As partners become more aware and accepting of their own complexities, they can relate more genuinely.

- Maintaining Individuality: While a relationship involves

a degree of merging, it's crucial to maintain individual interests, hobbies, and pursuits. This individuality enriches each partner and brings fresh energy and perspectives to the relationship.

- Supporting Each Other's Growth: Partners in a relationship should strive to be each other's allies in the journey of personal growth. This means encouraging each other's dreams, respecting each other's need for personal space, and being open to changes in each other.

- Communication and Boundaries: Open and honest communication is key to balancing individuation and intimacy. Discussing personal needs, boundaries, and growth helps in understanding each other better and fosters a supportive environment.

- Shared Goals and Values: While supporting individual paths, it's also important to have shared goals and values that bind the relationship. These commonalities create a sense of partnership and direction.

- Emotional Intimacy: Emotional intimacy should be nurtured along with personal growth. Sharing feelings, vulnerabilities, and insights from one's individuation process can deepen the emotional connection.

- Navigating Changes: As individuals grow, relationships inevitably change. Welcoming and adapting to these changes is part of maintaining a healthy, dynamic relationship.

- Role of Reflection and Adaptation: Regular reflection on how the balance is being maintained and adapting as necessary is crucial. This might involve periodic check-ins or couples' therapy.

In essence, balancing individuation and intimacy in a relationship is about nurturing a connection where both partners feel free to explore their true selves while maintaining a deep, empathetic bond with each other. This balance leads to a relationship that is not only supportive and loving but also vibrant with the growth and uniqueness of each partner.

Jung's Insights on Individuation Stages

Carl Jung's concept of individuation involves several stages, each representing a step towards achieving a fully integrated personality. Understanding these stages can provide valuable insights into personal development and how this growth intersects with and enriches romantic relationships.

- Confrontation with the Shadow: The first stage involves facing the shadow, the part of the psyche containing repressed ideas and instincts. Recognizing and accepting these hidden aspects is essential for growth. In relationships, this might mean acknowledging traits we dislike in ourselves rather than projecting them onto our partners.

- Dealing with the Persona: The persona is the social face presented to the world. This stage involves differentiating the persona from the true self. For couples, this might involve recognizing and moving beyond the roles they play in their relationship, revealing their more authentic selves to each other.

- Encounter with the Anima/Animus: Jung identified the anima and animus as the feminine and masculine aspects present in each individual, respectively. Integrating these aspects leads to a more balanced understanding of oneself and the opposite sex. In a relationship, this can deepen empathy and understanding between partners.

- Integration of the Self: The final stage is the integration of the Self, which represents the unity of the conscious and unconscious mind. Achieving this stage brings a sense of wholeness and authenticity. In relationships, this can manifest as a mature, grounded connection based on true understanding and acceptance.

- Continuous Process: It's important to note that individuation is a continuous, lifelong process. Each stage offers opportunities for learning and growth, both individually and within the context of a relationship.

- Challenges and Transformation: Each stage of individuation may present challenges, requiring introspection and sometimes difficult changes. For couples, navigating these challenges together can strengthen their bond and facilitate mutual growth.

- Impact on Relationships: As individuals progress through the stages of individuation, their relationships often become more genuine and profound. Partners who are engaged in their own individuation processes can support each other, leading to a dynamic and fulfilling partnership.

Jung's insights into the stages of individuation provide a roadmap for personal development. For couples, understanding and supporting each other through these stages can lead to a deepened connection and a more authentic, harmonious relationship.

***

- Turn to the corresponding section in *The Shadow Work Journal and Workbook for Couples* and complete the exercises. Reflect on your insights, apply the concepts, and explore your personal experiences. Taking this time for self-reflection will enhance your journey.

Moral Ambiguity

NAVIGATING ETHICAL COMPLEXITIES TOGETHER

> "The pendulum of the mind oscillates between sense and nonsense, not between right and wrong." — Carl Jung

Chapter 6, "Moral Ambiguity," delves into the complex intersection of morality, the shadow, and relationships. In life and love, situations often arise that lack clear-cut ethical answers, presenting us with moral ambiguities that challenge our understanding and decision-making. Carl Jung's insights into the human psyche offer a valuable perspective on navigating these gray areas, especially within the intimate context of a romantic relationship.

This chapter explores the concept of moral ambiguity through the lens of Jungian psychology, focusing on how couples can navigate ethical dilemmas and conflicting values. It examines how our shadow selves, those parts of us that we may not fully acknowledge or understand, can influence our moral judgments and interactions with our partners.

Understanding and addressing moral ambiguity is crucial for maintaining a healthy, honest, and mature relationship. It requires self-reflection, open communication, and a willingness to embrace the complexity of human nature. By exploring moral ambiguity together, couples can strengthen their bond, develop deeper empathy, and forge a more authentic connection based on mutual understanding and respect.

Exploring Moral Ambiguity in the Context of the Shadow

Moral ambiguity, when examined through the lens of Jungian psychology, often intertwines with the concept of the shadow—the unconscious part of our personality that contains repressed weaknesses, instincts, and desires. Exploring moral ambiguity in the context of the shadow is crucial for understanding the complexities of our moral decisions, particularly in intimate relationships.

- Shadow's Influence on Morality: The shadow often houses aspects of ourselves that we're not proud of or that conflict with our conscious moral values. This can include prejudiced thoughts, selfish desires, or aggressive impulses. These hidden aspects can significantly influence our moral judgments and behaviors.

- Projection of Moral Judgments: Just as we project unwanted aspects of our personality onto others, we can also project our moral ambiguities. For example, we might harshly judge a partner for behaviors or attitudes that, unconsciously, we find objectionable in ourselves.

- Reconciling Internal Conflicts: Moral ambiguity in the context of the shadow often stems from an internal conflict between our conscious values and unconscious desires or beliefs. Recognizing and reconciling these conflicts is key to personal growth and ethical development.

- Understanding Moral Complexity: Acknowledging the shadow helps in understanding the complexity of human morality. It allows us to see beyond black-and-white moral judgments and appreciate the nuances in ourselves and our partners.

- Empathy and Compassion: By exploring the shadow

side of our morality, we can develop greater empathy and compassion—both for ourselves and our partners. Understanding that we all grapple with moral ambiguities helps in fostering a more accepting and supportive relationship.

- Personal Growth and Relationship Dynamics: As individuals work through their moral ambiguities and shadow aspects, they often experience personal growth. This growth can lead to healthier and more honest relationship dynamics, where partners can discuss moral issues openly and without judgment.

- Navigating Ethical Dilemmas Together: For couples, exploring moral ambiguity together can be an opportunity to deepen their understanding of each other and strengthen their bond. It encourages honest discussions about values, ethics, and personal beliefs.

In summary, exploring moral ambiguity in the context of the shadow is a vital process for individuals and couples striving for authenticity and depth in their relationships. It involves facing uncomfortable truths, challenging personal biases, and developing a more nuanced understanding of morality and human behavior.

Navigating Ethical Dilemmas in Relationships

Navigating ethical dilemmas in relationships is a critical aspect of maintaining a healthy, respectful, and understanding partnership. These dilemmas often arise when partners face situations where their moral compasses point in different directions, or when individual values clash. Handling these situations effectively requires a delicate balance of communication, empathy, and mutual respect.

- Open and Honest Communication: The foundation for navigating ethical dilemmas is open and honest communication. Partners should feel safe to express their views, feelings, and concerns without fear of judgment. This includes discussing why certain issues are morally significant to each individual.

- Understanding and Respecting Differences: It's important to acknowledge that each partner may have different values and ethical perspectives. Understanding and respecting these differences is key, even if agreement isn't always possible.

- Empathy and Perspective-Taking: Trying to see the dilemma from the partner's point of view can be enlightening. Empathy allows individuals to appreciate the complexity of the issue and the emotions involved.

- Finding Common Ground: While some ethical dilemmas may not have a clear resolution, finding common ground or areas of agreement can help in reaching a compromise or understanding.

- Prioritizing the Relationship: In some instances, partners may choose to prioritize the health and well-being of their relationship over winning an ethical argument. This doesn't mean sacrificing one's values, but rather recognizing the value of the relationship itself.

- Seeking External Guidance: Sometimes, turning to a neutral third party like a therapist or counselor can help in navigating particularly challenging ethical dilemmas. They can provide a fresh perspective and mediate discussions.

- Reflecting on Personal Growth: Ethical dilemmas, while challenging, can be opportunities for personal and relational growth. They encourage individuals to reflect deeply on their values, beliefs, and the kind of relationship they aspire to have.

- Long-Term Solutions: In cases where ethical dilemmas are recurrent, it may be necessary to discuss long-term solutions or strategies to manage these disagreements in a healthy manner.

Navigating ethical dilemmas in relationships is not just about resolving conflicts; it's about growing closer through understanding, respect, and shared values. By effectively managing these challenges, couples can build a stronger, more resilient partnership.

Jung's Perspective on Morality and the Psyche

Carl Jung's perspective on morality is deeply intertwined with his concepts of the psyche and the collective unconscious. Jung did not view morality as a set of rigid rules imposed from the outside, but rather as an intrinsic aspect of the human psyche, evolving from both personal experiences and collective human history. His insights shed light on how morality plays out within individuals and, by extension, in their relationships.

- Morality as an Inner Experience: For Jung, morality is not just a social construct but an inner experience. He believed that moral understanding and behavior arise from the depths of the unconscious and are influenced by personal experiences and the collective unconscious.

- The Role of the Shadow in Morality: Jung viewed the shadow, which contains repressed ideas and impulses, as playing a crucial role in how individuals deal with moral issues. Acknowledging and integrating the shadow is vital for a genuine moral stance, as it prevents projecting one's moral shortcomings onto others.

- The Collective Unconscious and Morality: Jung's concept of the collective unconscious, a reservoir of human experiences and archetypes, suggests that our moral instincts are also influenced by shared human history and experiences. This collective aspect shapes our sense of right and wrong beyond personal and cultural experiences.

- Individuation and Moral Development: Jung saw the process of individuation, the integration of various aspects of the psyche, as key to moral development. Through this process, individuals develop a personal moral compass that is nuanced and deeply connected to their authentic selves.

- Ethical Relativism and Absolutism: Jung's approach to morality encompasses aspects of both ethical relativism and absolutism. While he recognized the subjective nature of moral experience, he also believed in certain universal ethical principles embedded in the collective unconscious.

- Moral Conflicts and Personal Growth: Jung believed that moral conflicts are essential for personal growth. Facing and wrestling with moral dilemmas is part of the journey towards psychological wholeness.

- Implications for Relationships: In the context of relationships, Jung's perspective on morality encourages partners to explore their own moral beliefs, understand their origins, and respect each other's moral viewpoints. This process can lead to deeper mutual understanding and a more authentic connection.

Understanding Jung's perspective on morality offers valuable insights into the complex nature of ethical beliefs and behaviors in personal and relational contexts. It encourages a deep, introspective approach to moral issues, fostering personal authenticity and relational harmony.

***

- Turn to the corresponding section in *The Shadow Work Journal and Workbook for Couples* and complete the exercises. Reflect on your insights, apply the concepts, and explore your personal experiences. Taking this time for self-reflection will enhance your journey.

Encounter With the Self

Discovering Authenticity for Deeper Intimacy

> "The privilege of a lifetime is to become who you truly are." — Carl Jung

Chapter 7, "Encounter with the Self," delves into one of the most profound and transformative concepts in Carl Jung's analytical psychology: the encounter with the Self. The 'Self' in Jungian terms represents the entirety of the psyche, encompassing both the conscious and the unconscious mind. It is the archetype of wholeness and the guiding force of the individuation process.

In this chapter, we explore the journey of encountering and understanding the true Self, a journey that is essential not only for personal growth but also for the deepening of intimate relationships. This process involves peeling back the layers of the persona (the social mask), integrating the shadow (the repressed aspects of the personality), and balancing the anima and animus (the feminine and masculine aspects within).

For couples, encountering the Self can be a powerful shared experience. It allows each partner to understand and embrace their full selves, leading to a more genuine and profound connection. This chapter will guide you through the stages of this encounter, offering insights into how this process can enhance both personal development and the dynamics of a romantic relationship. By engaging with the true Self, partners can foster a relationship that is deeply rooted in authenticity, mutual understanding, and empathic connection.

Encountering and Understanding the True Self

Encountering and understanding the true Self is a pivotal aspect of Jungian psychology and a crucial journey in personal development and relational depth. This process involves delving into the deepest parts of the psyche, beyond the conscious ego, to discover and embrace the core of who we truly are.
- The Concept of the True Self: In Jungian terms, the true Self is the center of the psyche, encompassing both the conscious and unconscious mind. It is the part of us that is authentic, unmasked by the persona (the social façade), and unswayed by the shadow (repressed aspects of our personality).

- The Journey to the True Self: Encountering the true Self is a journey that requires introspection, self-examination, and often, navigating through difficult emotional terrain. It involves confronting fears, biases, and illusions that we have about ourselves.

- Integrating the Unconscious: A significant part of understanding the true Self is integrating the unconscious aspects of the psyche. This includes recognizing and accepting the shadow, as well as understanding the role of dreams and symbols as messages from the unconscious.

- The Role of Individuation: The process of individuation, or becoming wholly oneself, is synonymous with encountering the true Self. It is about reconciling and harmonizing the various opposing aspects of the psyche.

- Implications for Relationships: In a romantic relationship, understanding one's true Self has profound implications. It allows for authenticity and honesty in the relationship and fosters a deeper connection as partners relate to each other's true selves, beyond social personas and projections.

- Challenges and Rewards: Encountering the true Self can be challenging as it may disrupt the status quo of one's self-perception and relationships. However, the rewards include a life lived with authenticity, deeper self-awareness, and more meaningful relationships.

- Practical Steps: Practical steps towards encountering the true Self include reflective practices such as journaling, meditation, creative expression, and active imagination exercises. These practices help in uncovering and integrating the various aspects of the Self.

Understanding and encountering the true Self is a transformative experience that leads to personal liberation and a profound understanding of one's place in the world and in relationships. This chapter guides you through this journey, illuminating the path to a deeper connection with yourself and your partner.

Jung's Theory of the Self and Its Relevance to Relationships

Carl Jung's theory of the Self is a cornerstone of his psychological framework, offering profound insights into personal development and its impact on relationships. The Self, in Jungian psychology, represents the central archetype of wholeness and the unification of the conscious and unconscious mind. Understanding this concept and its relevance to relationships is crucial for achieving deeper, more meaningful connections.

- The Self as a Guiding Force: Jung considered the Self to be the guiding force of the psyche, driving the process of individuation. It represents the fullest realization of our potential and is the source of our deepest motivations and aspirations.

- The Self vs. The Ego: Unlike the ego, which is the center of our conscious identity, the Self encompasses the totality of the psyche, including aspects of which we are not consciously aware. The ego's journey towards recognizing and aligning with the Self is key to personal growth.

- Balance and Wholeness: The Self seeks balance and wholeness, integrating the various conflicting aspects of the psyche, such as the persona, the shadow, and the anima/animus. This integration is essential for achieving a sense of completeness.

- Relevance to Relationships: In relationships, the journey towards the Self can have a significant impact. As individuals strive for self-realization and wholeness, they become more authentic and present in their relationships. This authenticity fosters deeper, more genuine connections.

- Projection and the Self: Understanding one's Self reduces the tendency to project unconscious aspects onto one's partner. This clarity allows for healthier interactions and more honest communication.

- Mutual Growth and Support: In a relationship, both partners can support each other's journey towards the Self. This mutual support fosters a relationship dynamic where both individuals can grow and flourish.

- Empathy and Understanding: Recognizing one's own complexities and struggles in the process of self-realization fosters empathy. Partners become more understanding and compassionate towards each other's journeys.

- Challenges and Opportunities: The path to realizing the Self can pose challenges in a relationship, as it often involves significant change and self-examination. However, these challenges present opportunities for strengthening the bond and deepening the connection.

Jung's theory of the Self elucidates the profound connection between personal growth and relationship dynamics. Encountering and aligning with the Self leads to more authentic and fulfilling relationships, characterized by mutual understanding, empathy, and support. This chapter explores how individuals and couples can navigate this journey, enriching both their personal lives and their shared experiences.

Personal Stories and Case Examples

To illustrate the profound impact of encountering the Self and its relevance to relationships, this section presents personal stories and case examples. These narratives provide real-life insights into how individuals navigate the journey toward self-realization and how this process influences their romantic partnerships.

Story of Emma and Lucas: Emma, a graphic designer, always struggled with expressing her true feelings, often wearing a persona that portrayed her as perpetually cheerful and agreeable. Through therapy and self-reflection, she began to encounter her true Self, realizing her need for deeper emotional connections. This journey transformed her relationship with Lucas, her partner, as she became more open and authentic, leading to a more genuine and fulfilling relationship.

- Case of Michael and Sarah: Michael, an accountant, was often dominated by his persona at work, carrying this over into his home life. His journey towards encountering his true Self revealed a more creative and sensitive side. As he embraced these aspects, his relationship with Sarah became richer, with shared creative pursuits and deeper emotional intimacy.

- Anna's Journey to Self-Discovery: Single at the time, Anna's journey towards encountering her true Self involved reconciling with her shadow aspects, including her fear of vulnerability. This process prepared her for a healthier future relationship, as she learned to be more open and true to her feelings.

- Transformation of Alex and Jamie: Alex and Jamie, both deeply committed to personal growth, supported each other's journeys toward self-realization. This mutual support helped them navigate changes in their relationship dynamics, fostering a deeper understanding and appreciation of each other's true selves.

- Therapeutic Insights from Dr. Brown: Dr. Brown, a Jungian therapist, shares insights from her practice, detailing how clients who engage with their true Self often see transformative effects in their relationships. She notes that these individuals develop a clearer sense of what they need and desire in a partner, leading to more authentic and satisfying relationships.

These stories and cases exemplify the transformative power of encountering and understanding the true Self. They highlight how this journey not only fosters personal growth and self-awareness but also profoundly enriches and deepens romantic relationships. Through these narratives, readers can gain inspiration and insight into their own journeys toward self-realization and its impact on their partnerships.

***

- Turn to the corresponding section in *The Shadow Work Journal and Workbook for Couples* and complete the exercises. Reflect on your insights, apply the concepts, and explore your personal experiences. Taking this time for self-reflection will enhance your journey.

Transformation

NAVIGATING PERSONAL CHANGE AND RELATIONSHIP GROWTH

> "I am not what happened to me, I am what I choose to become."
> — Carl Jung

Chapter 8, "Transformation," delves into the dynamic and often profound changes that individuals and couples experience through the processes of shadow work, individuation, and encountering the Self. Transformation in the Jungian context is not merely about change; it represents a deep and fundamental shift in how individuals understand themselves and relate to others, especially their partners.

In the realm of relationships, transformation can manifest in numerous ways: from the way partners communicate and understand each other to the fundamental dynamics of the relationship itself. This chapter explores the nature of transformation, how it originates from deep self-awareness and integration of the unconscious, and its profound impact on romantic partnerships.

The journey of transformation is both personal and shared within a relationship. As individuals evolve, grow, and change, their relationships inevitably do as well. Understanding and navigating these transformations is crucial for maintaining a healthy, vibrant, and deeply connected relationship. This chapter will guide you through the transformative processes and their implications for relationships, offering insights into how couples can embrace and support each other through these changes.

The Transformative Power of Shadow Work

Shadow work, a concept central to Carl Jung's analytical psychology, refers to the process of exploring and integrating the unconscious aspects of the personality, often termed the 'shadow'. This work is inherently transformative, both for individuals and for their relationships.

- Unveiling the Unconscious: Shadow work involves bringing to light the hidden parts of ourselves—traits, emotions, and memories that have been repressed. This unveiling is often the first step in a profound transformation, as it allows individuals to confront aspects of themselves they have long ignored or denied.

- Enhanced Self-Awareness and Authenticity: As individuals engage with their shadow, they develop a deeper understanding of themselves. This enhanced self-awareness leads to greater authenticity in how they present themselves and interact with others, including their partners.

- Reduction of Projection in Relationships: One of the transformative effects of shadow work in relationships is the reduction of projection—attributing one's own unacceptable qualities to their partner. By owning and integrating these qualities, individuals can interact with their partners more honestly and constructively.

- Improved Communication and Empathy: Understanding one's shadow can lead to improved communication and empathy in relationships. Individuals who recognize their own flaws and struggles are often better equipped to understand and empathize with their partner's challenges.

- Resolution of Internal Conflicts: Shadow work often involves resolving internal conflicts that can affect emotional well-being and relationship dynamics. By reconciling these conflicts, individuals can find a greater sense of inner peace and stability.

- Personal Growth and Relationship Evolution: The personal growth that comes from shadow work can lead to significant changes in relationship dynamics. Partners may find that as they evolve, their relationship deepens, becoming more resilient and fulfilling.

- Empowerment and Self-Acceptance: Engaging with the shadow can be an empowering experience. It encourages individuals to accept all parts of themselves, fostering a sense of wholeness that they bring into their relationships.

- Navigating Challenges Together: For couples, jointly engaging in shadow work or supporting each other's individual journeys can be a powerful way to navigate the challenges and changes of a relationship, strengthening the bond between them.

In summary, the transformative power of shadow work is profound and far-reaching. It not only catalyzes personal growth and self-understanding but also significantly enhances the quality and depth of romantic relationships. This chapter underscores the importance of embracing the shadow as a path to a more authentic, empathetic, and connected partnership.

Changes in Relationships Through Self-Awareness and Growth

The journey of self-awareness and personal growth inevitably brings about changes in relationships. As individuals evolve, so do their interactions, expectations, and dynamics with their partners. This transformation, often a result of engaging in processes like shadow work and individuation, can have profound implications for a romantic partnership.

- Deepening of Emotional Intimacy: As individuals gain self-awareness, they become more open and vulnerable with their partners. This vulnerability can lead to deeper emotional intimacy, where partners share not just their joys and successes but also their fears, insecurities, and weaknesses.

- Shift in Communication Patterns: Increased self-awareness often leads to more effective and honest communication. Partners who understand themselves better are able to express their needs and feelings more clearly, reducing misunderstandings and conflicts.

- Redefining Relationship Dynamics: Personal growth can lead to a redefinition of relationship roles and dynamics. As individuals change, they may seek different things from the relationship, leading to a shift in how partners relate to and support each other.

- Enhanced Empathy and Understanding: Self-awareness fosters empathy, enabling partners to better understand each other's perspectives and experiences. This understanding can create a more compassionate and supportive relationship environment.

- Resolution of Past Issues: Personal growth often involves addressing and resolving past issues, which can have a positive impact on relationships. By dealing with personal baggage, individuals can prevent past patterns from negatively affecting their current relationship.

- Balancing Independence and Interdependence: With self-growth, individuals often find a better balance between their need for independence and their desire for a connected, interdependent relationship. This balance is crucial for a healthy, fulfilling partnership.

- Increased Flexibility and Adaptability: Growth can lead to greater flexibility and adaptability in relationships. Partners who are committed to growth and self-improvement are often more open to change and better equipped to navigate life's inevitable challenges together.

- New Shared Experiences and Growth Opportunities: As both partners grow, they can explore new experiences and opportunities for growth together, which can bring excitement and vitality to the relationship.

The changes brought about by self-awareness and personal growth can strengthen and enrich a relationship. However, they can also present challenges, as adjustments and accommodations may be needed. Embracing these changes with openness, understanding, and a commitment to mutual growth can lead to a more authentic, resilient, and deeply connected partnership.

Drawing from Jung's Transformative Concepts

Carl Jung's transformative concepts provide a rich framework for understanding personal growth and its impact on relationships. These concepts, deeply rooted in the exploration of the unconscious, individuation, and the integration of the self, offer valuable insights into the transformative journey of individuals and couples.

- The Process of Individuation: Jung's concept of individuation, the process of becoming aware of oneself and achieving a sense of wholeness, is central to transformation. In relationships, this process can lead to both partners developing a stronger sense of self, which in turn can create a more authentic and balanced partnership.

- Integration of the Shadow: The integration of the shadow, or the unconscious aspects of the personality, is a transformative experience. Recognizing and accepting these hidden parts can lead to significant personal growth and a deeper understanding in relationships, reducing projection and misunderstanding.

- Embracing Opposites: Jung emphasized the importance of embracing opposites within the psyche, such as the anima and animus (the feminine and masculine aspects). Understanding and integrating these aspects can lead to a more harmonious internal state and improve interactions with one's partner.

- Role of Symbols and Dreams: Jungian psychology places great importance on symbols and dreams as vehicles for understanding the unconscious mind. In relationships, exploring these symbols and dreams together can provide insights into each partner's inner world, fostering deeper connection and empathy.

- Transformation Through Transcendence: Jung believed in the transformative power of transcending beyond the ego. In a relationship, this might mean moving beyond individual needs and desires to embrace the needs of the partnership, leading to a more selfless and compassionate connection.

- Collective Unconscious and Shared Experiences: The concept of the collective unconscious highlights shared human experiences and archetypes. In relationships, understanding these shared human patterns can provide a sense of unity and connectedness.

- Confronting the Self: The ultimate goal of Jung's transformative journey is the confrontation with the Self – an experience that leads to the realization of one's full potential. For couples, this can mean supporting each other in reaching their fullest potential, both individually and together.

Drawing from Jung's transformative concepts, individuals and couples can gain profound insights into their growth journey. These concepts offer tools for navigating the complexities of personal and relational transformation, ultimately leading to more fulfilling and authentic partnerships.

***

- Turn to the corresponding section in *The Shadow Work Journal and Workbook for Couples* and complete the exercises. Reflect on your insights, apply the concepts, and explore your personal experiences. Taking this time for self-reflection will enhance your journey.

Afterword

Reflecting on the Journey

As we reach the conclusion of this exploration into the depths of Jungian psychology and its application to relationships, it's time to reflect on the journey we've undertaken. From delving into the unconscious and confronting repressed desires to understanding projection, embracing the process of integration, and navigating the complex path of individuation, each chapter has offered insights into the intricate dynamics of personal growth and its profound impact on romantic relationships.

This journey has not only been about understanding theoretical concepts; it has been a practical exploration of how these ideas manifest in our daily lives and intimate partnerships. We've seen how shadow work can transform our understanding of ourselves and our partners, how individuation can lead to a more authentic and fulfilling relationship, and how facing moral ambiguities can strengthen the bonds of trust and empathy.

As we conclude, it's important to recognize that the journey of self-discovery and relational growth is ongoing. The insights and lessons learned are not final destinations but stepping stones to deeper understanding and connection.

In this conclusion, we'll summarize the key takeaways from each chapter and reflect on how to continue applying these insights to nurture and enrich your relationship. The journey of exploring the self and navigating the complexities of a partnership is a continuous adventure—one that can lead to a profoundly rewarding and deeply connected shared life.

Summarizing Key Insights and Takeaways

As we conclude our journey through the realms of Jungian psychology and its application to relationships, it's essential to consolidate the key insights and takeaways:

- The Unconscious Mind: Understanding the unconscious is fundamental to self-awareness and relationship dynamics. Recognizing its influence helps in addressing deep-rooted behaviors and patterns.

- Repressed Desires: Acknowledging and integrating repressed desires can significantly enhance personal fulfillment and relationship satisfaction. It's about bringing hidden aspects to light and dealing with them constructively.

- Projection in Relationships: Identifying and managing projections are crucial for authentic interactions. Recognizing our projections helps in reducing misunderstandings and fostering empathy.

- Integration of the Shadow: Embracing the shadow leads to a more complete self-understanding and reduces the strain on relationships caused by unconscious behaviors.

- Individuation: The journey towards individuation enhances personal integrity and authenticity in relationships, fostering deeper connections.

- Moral Ambiguity: Navigating moral ambiguities requires open communication, empathy, and a willingness to understand different perspectives, strengthening the relationship.

- Encounter with the Self: Encountering and understanding the true Self is pivotal for personal growth and the development of genuine relationships.

- Transformation: Personal and relational transformation is a continual process, fueled by ongoing self-awareness, growth, and adaptation to changes.

The Ongoing Journey of Shadow Work in Relationships

Shadow work in relationships is an ongoing process. It involves continuous reflection, open dialogue, and a commitment to understanding both the self and the partner. This work enhances not only personal growth but also the depth and quality of the relationship.

As you move forward, remember that personal and relational growth is a perpetual journey. Embrace the lessons learned, and continue to apply these insights to nurture your relationship. Encourage and support each other in your individual paths of growth and self-discovery. The journey is as rewarding as it is challenging, and it paves the way for a deeply connected, authentic, and fulfilling partnership.

In conclusion, the insights from Jungian psychology offer valuable tools for understanding and enriching both personal development and romantic relationships. By continuing to engage with these concepts, you can build a relationship that is not only loving but also deeply rooted in mutual understanding, growth, and authenticity.

THANK YOU

for getting this book and for making it all the way to the end!

Before you go, I wanted to ask you for one small favor. Could you please consider posting a review?

Because posting a review is the best and easiest way to support the work of independent authors like me.

Your feedback will help me a ton!

>>Leave a review on Amazon US<<

AFTERWORD

The Ultimate Self-Help Narcissistic Abuse Recovery Book

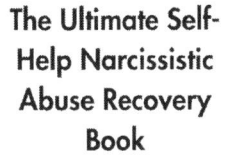

Narcissistic Abuse Recovery

Childhood Trauma and Recovery

Healing Your Inner Child
(Childhood Trauma and Recovery Workbook)

CALLIE PARKER
SHADOW
WORK
FOR COUPLES
A Guide to Strengthen Your Relationship, Build Trust and Understanding, and Cultivate Lasting Love

THE
SHADOW
WORK
JOURNAL AND
WORKBOOK
FOR COUPLES
CALLIE PARKER

Shadow
Work
for
Teens
A Guide for Teenagers and Young Adults to Overcome Inner Challenges, Build Confidence, and Practice Self-Love
CALLIE PARKER

The
Shadow
Work
Journal
for
Teens
Guided Prompts and Activities for Inner Healing, Building Confidence, and Practicing Self-Love
CALLIE PARKER

CALLIE PARKER
SHADOW
WORK
LGBTQ+
EDITION
A Guide to Inner Healing and Self-Love

CALLIE PARKER
THE
SHADOW
WORK JOURNAL
LGBTQ+
EDITION

Printed in Great Britain
by Amazon